Start-up: A Beginners Guide to Launching a Successful Online Business

Tabatha Adjonteh

Copyright © 2014 Tabatha Adjonteh

All rights reserved.

ISBN: 1505560179
ISBN-13: 978-1505560176

This book or any portion thereof may not be reproduced or used in any manner whatsoever without the express written permission of the publisher
except for the use of brief quotations in a book review.

Printed in the United States of America

First Printing, December 2014

Contact Information:

Tabatha Adjonteh

Website: www.tabathaadjonteh.com

Email: tabathaadjonteh@gmail.com

Phone: 213-534-6544

DEDICATION

To all of those pursuing financial freedom and control of your 24 hour day, this book is dedicated to you.

CONTENTS

1 Find Your Niche

2 Getting Down to Business

3 Raising Capital

4 Budgeting

5 Marketing

1 FIND YOUR NICHE

Each morning people wake up and choose how they will start the day. For some, this may mean a quick workout before heading to the office and for others it could mean spending some time with their kids, reading the morning news or catching up on work-related emails. I believe that having a home-based online business can give you the freedom to do the things that you love.

First thing is to find out what you are born to do. Just because you have a passion for something does not mean that you are suppose to be doing it. It's great to have passion because your passion is your drive to do what you love, but it must be your niche. If I want to be a singer and can't sing, it will never come into fruition unless I am singing to the deaf. I say this with no pun intended. These are some steps from Forbes that I have personally utilized to help me to find my niche:

Listen to your heart. Follow your heart, not just your reason. You seldom go wrong when you listen to your own inner voice.

Get out of your comfort zone. Golden opportunities often lie just outside our comfort zone. Have the courage and fortitude to grab that brass ring.

Avoid analysis paralysis. Do your homework, but ultimately you need to take action.

Somehow the biggest risk is not to risk at all. Don't wait for your ship to come in… row out and meet it.

Don't wait for the perfect time. There will never be a truly perfect time to act. In life, you generally learn more by doing than waiting. The perfect time to act is now!

Face your fears. Feel the fear and do it anyway. Have the courage to work through your fear and use it to propel your spirit and rekindle your focus.

Live in the present. Make the present the primary focus in your life, not the past or the future. Remember, life is a gift; that's why they call it a present. The present moment is all you'll ever have in your life.

Take the leap. Aristotle once said, "Courage is the first of all human qualities because it is the one that guarantees all others." Have the courage to take the leap and close the gap between your dreams and reality.

In business, a successful strategy offers a clarion call to action. But an action strategy often requires a certain degree of risk. Once a company completes its market research with due diligence, it's time to pull the ripcord. Similarly, in life, it's not good enough to just have a mission. We need to act. When was the last time you risked failure for something you passionately believed in?

Are you willing to let go of what others will think, and honor your God-given gift instead? Take a moment right now to complete the following questions in a journal or notebook. They will help you clear the many voices in your head, so you and your niche can emerge…

* I would complete my dream, except that my father....
* When I think of my dream, I think of my mother....
* Everyone keeps telling me....
* I don't pursue my dreams because....
* The truth about my dreams is that....
* If I could truly do anything I wanted to in life, I would....

Make sure that you know and are clear on your vision, values and goals. It helps you see when there are opportunities that fit in with that vision. It keeps you from going on a path that is not consistent with what you believe in.

Identify your passion and where it fits. To do this, consider what you're passionate about in your career. What tasks energize you rather than drain you? What are you working on when you get "in your zone" or "in the flow?" What professional areas could you continue exploring without growing bored? Those are the things you should be pursuing as you consider your career path.

Know your strengths and develop your own style. Figure out what works for you and work to mold the process to align with your strengths. Don't look at how others succeed and try to emulate their approach if it doesn't play to your skills.

Know what you are good at and what you are not good at. If the online business involves something you truly can't—or don't want to—develop, move on. It's not the right one for you. Not yet sure of your weaknesses? Consult again with that trusted manager, mentor, or coworker. If you can convince them that your request is sincere, they'll tell you!

Now, take this advice, and put it all together to identify your ideal career. Ask yourself: What could you be doing more of in your career that aligns with your values, passions, and strengths? Is there something you're great at—something you could do in your own leadership style?

Is it possible to maneuver into a role or career path that combines all of that, while delivering a highly valued service to your company or industry that will make you a sought-after resource?

If so, that's your niche. And it's what's likely to make you happier in your career than anything else. So before you take your next step up the corporate ladder, or an entrepreneur, make sure the deepest parts with you (your spirit) agrees with your decision.

2 GETTING DOWN TO BUSINESS

There is a proven sequence of steps you can follow to guarantee your success when you're starting a small business online:

- ❖ Find a need and fill it.
- ❖ Write copy that sells.
- ❖ Design and build an easy-to-use website.
- ❖ Use search engines to drive traffic to your site.
- ❖ Establish an expert reputation for yourself.
- ❖ Follow up with your customers and subscribers with e-mail.
- ❖ Increase your income through back-end sales and upselling.

Most people who are just starting out make the mistake of looking for a product first, and a market second. To boost your chances of success, start with a market. The trick is to find a group of people who are searching for a solution to a problem, but not finding many results. The internet makes this kind of market research easy:

- o Visit online forums to see what questions people ask and what problems they're trying to solve.
- o Do keyword research to find keywords that a lot of people are searching, but for which not many sites are competing.
- o Check out your potential competitors by visiting their sites and taking note of what they're doing to fill the demand. Then you can use what you've learned and create a product for a market that

already exists--and do it better than the competition.

There's a proven sales copy formula that takes visitors through the selling process from the moment they arrive to the moment they make a purchase:

- ➤ Arouse interest with a compelling headline.
- ➤ Describe the problem your product solves.
- ➤ Establish your credibility as a solver of this problem.
- ➤ Add testimonials from people who have used your product.
- ➤ Talk about the product and how it benefits the user.
- ➤ Make an offer.
- ➤ Make a strong guarantee.
- ➤ Create urgency.
- ➤ Ask for the sale.

Throughout your copy, you need to focus on how your product or service is uniquely able solve people's problems or make their lives better. Think like a customer and ask "What's in it for me?"

Once you've got your market and product, and you've nailed down your selling process, now you're ready for your small-business web design. Remember to keep it simple. You have fewer than five seconds to grab someone's attention--otherwise they're gone, never to be seen again. Some important tips to keep in mind:

1. Choose one or two plain fonts on a white background.
2. Make your navigation clear, simple, and the same on every page.

3. Only use graphics, audio or video if they enhance your message.
4. Include an opt-in offer so you can collect e-mail addresses.
5. Make it easy to buy--no more than two clicks between potential customer and checkout.
6. Your website is your online storefront, so make it customer-friendly.

Pay-per-click advertising is the easiest way to get traffic to a brand-new site. It has two advantages over waiting for the traffic to come to you organically. First, PPC ads show up on the search pages immediately, and second, PPC ads allow you to test different keywords, as well as headlines, prices and selling approaches. Not only do you get immediate traffic, but you can also use PPC ads to discover your best, highest-converting keywords. Then you can distribute the keywords throughout your site in your copy and code, which will help your rankings in the organic search results.

People use the internet to find information. Provide that information for free to other sites, and you'll see more traffic and better search engine rankings. The secret is to always include a link to your site with each tidbit of information.

- ✓ Give away free, expert content. Create articles, videos or any other content that people will find useful. Distribute that content through online article directories or social media sites.
- ✓ Include "send to a friend" links on valuable content on your website.
- ✓ Become an active expert in industry forums and social networking sites where your target market hangs out.

You'll reach new readers. But even better, every site that posts your content will link back to yours. Search engines love links from relevant sites and will reward you in the rankings.

When you build an opt-in list, you're creating one of the most valuable assets of your online business. Your customers and subscribers have given you permission to send them e-mail. That means:

a) You're giving them something they've asked for.
b) You're developing lifetime relationships with them.
c) The response is 100 percent measurable.
d) E-mail marketing is cheaper and more effective than print, TV or radio because it's highly targeted.
e) Anyone who visits your site and opts in to your list is a very hot lead. And there's no better tool than e-mail for following up with those leads.

One of the most important internet marketing strategies is to develop every customer's lifetime value. At least 36 percent of people who have purchased from you once will buy from you again if you follow up with them. Closing that first sale is by far the most difficult part--not to mention the most expensive. So use back-end selling and upselling to get them to buy again:

- ✓ Offer products that complement their original purchase.
- ✓ Send out electronic loyalty coupons they can redeem on their next visit.
- ✓ Offer related products on your "Thank You" page after they purchase.

Reward your customers for their loyalty and they'll become even more loyal. The internet changes so fast that one year online equals about five years in the real world. But the principles of how to start and grow a successful online business haven't changed at all. If you're just starting a small business online, stick to this sequence. If you've been online awhile, do a quick review and see if there's a step you're neglecting, or never got around to doing in the first place. You can't go wrong with the basics.

You have to be willing to do the work and put the hours in at the beginning. Ask yourself this. Are you working a few more hours to pay off bills or are you working a few more hours to build wealth for your family? Which one makes it a little easier to work the extra hours?

If you face north, you will go in that direction. If you face despair and disappointment, your life will play out in that fashion. But if you face hope and opportunity, your life will follow that course.

If you take action now, you will reap the results later. Just because everybody can do something worthwhile does not mean that everyone will. You have what it takes to work hard and achieve more, but not everyone will work hard. Most humans take the path of least resistance. Don't be like everybody. Changing your life means doings things others choose not to do.

Because of the problems people experience in life, some become conditioned to believe that the current troubles are all that life has to offer. They don't know they can make a change and so they don't. Sometimes making a change can be as simple as reading a book, taking a class, going to a seminar or seeking better knowledge.

What if everything you touched turned to gold and everything that came your way got better or cleaner than you found it? What would that do for your psyche? In every area of your life and business, develop the mindset that because you touched it, it will only get better.

Yes there will be some disappointment in your new endeavor, but don't let anything make you give up. You may have to tweak a few things, but again don't give up. If a professional football player fumbles the ball, he needs to get that play out of his mind so he can concentrate on the next play. Yes, it was disappointing, but he has to put it in perspective. In life, you can't let little things cheat you out of big opportunities down the line.

Set some daily goals to insure you are using your time wisely. If you're not careful, sometimes simply being busy all the time can fool you. You may feel as if you're getting a lot accomplished, but when you take a step back you just might see that you are indeed moving, but not in the right direction. Don't be busy just for the sake of being busy. Make sure you are moving toward achieving your goals.

3 RAISING CAPITAL

Whether you've been in business one week or five years, an infusion of funds is always welcome. But what type of financing is best for your business? There are so many factors to consider--from the stage of your business to how much it'll cost to get the money--that just choosing a path to follow can be overwhelming.

When you are just starting out, you're not at the point yet where a traditional lender or investor would be interested in you. So that leaves you with selling cherished assets, borrowing against your home, maxing out credit cards, dipping into a 401(k), and asking loved ones for loans. There is a lot of risk involved, including the risk of bankruptcy with your personal finances and soured relationships with friends and family.

This is the hard part behind starting a business -- putting so much at risk. But doing so is the rite of passage to both success and failure. It's what sets entrepreneurs apart from people who collect paychecks.

A major key is to ramp up initial operations as quickly as possible to get to the point where outside investors can see and feel the venture, as well as understand that you took some risk getting it to that point.

Some businesses can also be bootstrapped. They can be built up quickly enough to make money without aid from investors who might otherwise come in and start calling the shots.

With so much at risk, it is important to have a strong business plan in place, and to seek out advice from experienced entrepreneurs and experts -- people who might also invest in your business someday.

Seek out local entrepreneurship advice programs. One place to start looking is the SBA's website, which has a search engine for finding local Small Business Development Centers, SCORE chapters and other resources

Many people are not borrowing money from banks anymore because there are other options. They are using other resources. Here are a few ideas:

Startup founders, take note: If you want to raise funds from angel investors or venture capitalists to grow your business, it recently became much easier to do so.

On Sept. 23, part of the JOBS Act went into effect, lifting the ban on general solicitation. This means that instead of being forced to seek introductions to potential investors privately, companies may publicly express their interest in equity fundraising.

Because the U.S. Securities and Exchange Commission maintains strict rules regarding whom you may solicit for investment funds, online fundraising platforms may be the simplest (and safest) option. Here are four leading investor-company matchmaking platforms to consider.

AngelList — This minimalist website allows startups and investors to search for the opportunities that are most relevant to them. Startups may post details about their founding team, a brief summary of their business, and details about their fundraising plans (available only to accredited investors).

Startups may also post job openings and use the platform to recruit potential employees. Investors, once approved, may search for startups based on location, industry, name, funding level, and other criteria. Startups pay nothing to get listed; investors pay 5 percent of their investment's value to AngelList. AngelList alums, which include GetAround, Artsy, and Life360, have raised more than $2.9 billion to date.

Fundable — This site is similar to the crowdfunding platform Kickstarter, but in addition to allowing fans to donate specific amounts in exchange for rewards, the site enables investors to provide funds in exchange for shares of stock. Fundable charges startups $99 a month, plus a 3.5 percent processing fee for credit-card transactions. Although the option to solicit investors is new, some companies have already achieved substantial success: Ube, an app that allows users to control your home's lighting via smartphone, has raised $925,000 through the platform to date.

Gust — This platform, previously known as AngelSoft, exclusively focuses on matching entrepreneurs with accredited investors. To that end, Gust offers a variety of tools for developing effective VC pitches. You can use the site to create both public and private business profiles, to put together a video pitch, to search for investors, and to track investors' activity on the site. Gust is free to entrepreneurs, and investors pay a fee that is not publicly disclosed.

The site's 1,000-plus investment groups have funded more than 1,800 startups in the past year. Pressly, a mobile startup, recently used Gust to solicit introductions and invitations to events; the founders credit the site with helping them raise $1.5 million.

Startups.co — With more than 300,000 companies and 20,000 investors in its stable, Startups.co is one of the largest platforms through which entrepreneurs and investors can "meet and mingle." The platform is largely entrepreneur-focused, offering tools and expert consultants to help business owners create pitches and find investors.

That level of service comes at a cost, however: The platform charges entrepreneurs $59 per month for access to its network of investors, plus flat-rate fees (starting around $300) for consulting services; there are no disclosed fees for investors to participate. The platform provides opportunities for businesses seeking both large and small investments: One music label received $1.5 million in funding through the site.

4 BUDGETING

Budgets are the roadmaps for your business' future. With clear departmental and company-wide budgets in place, everyone on the team knows the goals you are trying to reach and the parameters they have to work within. They can measure their success or failure relative to the standard at any given time, adjusting throughout the year as needed in order to ensure business goals are met or exceeded.

Creating a budget doesn't have to be a daunting task. In fact, it can be pretty simple, but more importantly, it can be an eye-opening experience. You can learn more about your business and what you can do to reach your goals by walking through the budgeting process.

You can create all the budgets you want, but if no one is paying attention to them, or if they are created in a vacuum, it's wasted effort. Before delivering budgetary guidelines, you must first identify and communicate your goals. Here's the thing, though, they need to be realistic and based on a number of factors.

Here are three tips to help you get started, followed by a brief guide to constructing a solid budget that works for your business:

I. Start with what you want at the end of the day (cash).

We can have all the goals we want, but if we don't

have the cash to pay ourselves and support our families, those goals are moot. Make sure you know how much cash you need each month to operate, so you can carve that out first before you spend any money on items that are not absolutely necessary to day-to-day operations.

II. List your projected expenses, starting with fixed ones.

If you've been in business for any period of time, you should have a good idea of what your fixed expenses will be for the upcoming year. Fixed expenses are those that do not change with fluctuations in revenue, sales or production. These include things like rent, insurance, dues and, depending on your industry, salaries.

III. List Your Expected Variable Expenses

Unlike fixed costs, variable expenses can increase or decrease based on the activity of your business. For example, expenses for a manufacturing company would have to account for higher costs of raw materials as the company's production levels rise. On the other hand, for a professional services firm, it could involve higher payroll expenses if you have higher revenue and need to expand your team (more work, more people to do it).

Based on the goals you have set, the company's past patterns and the trends in the industry, what variable expenses do you anticipate your company will encounter in the coming year?

When that's figured out, determine what percentage of revenue your variable expenses are. You can do this by dividing the variable expenses from a 12-month period by the overall revenue from the same period. Keep this figure handy, as you'll need this percentage later.

IV. Build in Your Projected Revenue

Once you've identified and listed all of your anticipated expenses, it's time to talk about how much money you expect to bring in to the company. When you were identifying your goals earlier, you probably thought about how you were going to meet them, so here's where the proverbial rubber hits the road.

How much revenue do you expect to bring in each month and for the year? If possible, break it down by department or product line, so you can get a truly realistic picture of where your revenue will come from for the year.

Plug these numbers into your budget. Here is the basic format you should use:

Projected Revenue − Variable Expenses − Fixed Expenses = Projected Net Income

Now for the moment of truth: Does your projected net income equal how much cash you need at the end of the day? If not, what can be done to fix that? Are there additional ways to decrease your variable expenses or increase your revenue that you haven't tried yet?

Often the budgeting process can uncover amazing opportunities or issues that need to be addressed. Don't allow yourself to be alarmed or overwhelmed. You're revealing valuable information that will help you make informed decisions and ensure that your company is as financially strong as it can be.

V. Use the Budget!

To get the most from your budget, you must be sure to use it. Don't just create it and shove it in a drawer. Stick with it and update it as needed throughout the year. While you spent time anticipating the upcoming year's influence on your budget, no one has a crystal ball. Updates are necessary and expected from time to time. Review where you actually are compared to your projections, and make changes as needed.

A simple budget versus actual report can be generated in most accounting systems. The fact that you have a plan to use for comparison and measurement is a powerful advantage. You'll be amazed by the insight and control that this information will provide, and how it allows you to make better decisions and adjust to change as it occurs.

5 MARKETING

Last but not least is marketing. Let's learn how to get paid from all of our hard work. Along with the marketing ideas I gave you in a previous chapter, I will give you a list of low-cost ways to market as well, seeing that finances can be an issue to new business owners.

The Internet has drastically altered the way in which information is shared, and has had a profound impact on marketing. Over the past few years, there has been more of a shift toward inbound techniques, while many outbound tactics have become antiquated. More businesses are finding success publishing original content rather than embedding advertisements within external content, because of the additional benefits these tactics offer, such as branding and audience growth.

- **Create business cards that prospects keep.**

Most business cards are tossed within hours of a meeting. Instead of having your card tossed, create one that recipients actually will use—say, a good-looking notepad with your contact info and tagline on every page.

- **Develop an electronic mailing list and send old-fashioned letters.**

Most businesses have harnessed the power of e-newsletters—and you definitely should be sending out one, too. It's very cost-effective. But because email marketing is now nearly ubiquitous, you can quickly stand out by occasionally sending personal, surface-mail letters to customers and prospects. Just make sure the letter delivers something customers want to read, whether it's an analysis of recent events in your field, premium offers, or a sweetener personalized for the recipient (a discount on the customer's next purchase of whatever was last purchased, for instance). This mailing has to have value to those that read it, so it reflects the value of what you offer.

- **Boost your profile at trade shows and conferences.**

You can quickly create signage, glossy postcards with your contact information, product news inserts, or an event mini-website—all with Microsoft Publisher. With Office 365, you'll also have a hosted external website for your business, at no extra cost.

- **Combine business with pleasure—and charity.**

Spearhead an event, party, or conference for a cause you care about. That puts you in the position of getting to know lots of people and shows off your small-business leadership skills.

- **Become an online expert.**

This is the "free sample" approach to bringing in business. Research active email discussion lists and online bulletin boards that are relevant to your business and audience. Join several and start posting expert advice to solve problems or answer questions. You may need to keep this up for a bit. But the rewards come back in paying clients and referrals.

- **Local media**

Editorial features convey more credibility with prospective clients than paid advertising does. To get coverage from the local media, whether from the town newspaper, TV or radio stations, or from trade journals, you need a fresh, timely story. It's usually worthwhile to hire an experienced publicist to position the stories, target appropriate media representative, and write and send press releases. Usually, you can work on a short-term or contingency basis.

- **Finally, don't let customers simply slip away.**

Make an effort to reel them back in. It costs a lot less to retain a disgruntled or inactive customer than to acquire a new one. If you haven't heard from a customer in a while, send a personalized email (you can automate this process), inquiring whether all is well. For a customer who suffered a bad experience, pick up the phone, acknowledging the unpleasantness and ask if there's anything you can do. A discount can't hurt either. Being kind to customers is the smartest low-cost marketing you can do.

ABOUT THE AUTHOR

Tabatha has been writing since the age of twelve. She studied business management at Liberty University and accounting as well. Her literary career began at Regent University where she studied cinematography. She believes that her writing is a form of worship to God, which allows her to draw closer to him. When not writing she enjoys spending time with her family, watching old movies, traveling and mentoring young women.

May the peace of God, which passeth all understanding keep your hearts and minds through Christ Jesus. Amen.

www.ingramcontent.com/pod-product-compliance
Lightning Source LLC
Chambersburg PA
CBHW051828170526
45167CB00005B/2201